D1531165

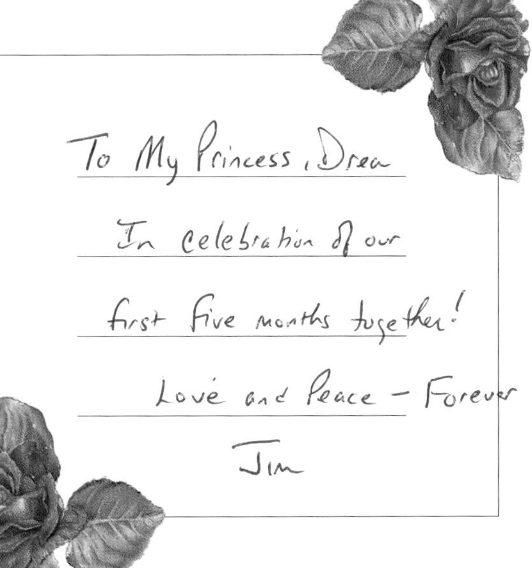

To My Princess, Drea

In celebration of our

first five months together!

Love and Peace - Forever

Jim

Victoria

The Romantic Heart

THE ROMANTIC HEART

HEARST BOOKS
New York

All permissions and copyright credits appear on pages 138-143. Recognizing the importance of preserving what has been written, it is the policy of William Morrow and Company, Inc., and its imprints and affiliates to have the books it publishes printed on acid-free paper, and we exert our best efforts to that end.

ISBN: 0-688-12589-1

Printed in Singapore
First U. S. Edition
1 2 3 4 5 6 7 8 9 10

For Victoria—
Nancy Lindemeyer, Editor-in-Chief
Bryan E. McCay, Art Director
John Mack Carter, Director, Magazine Development

Edited by Linda Sunshine
Designed by Nina Ovryn
Produced by Smallwood & Stewart, Inc., New York City

Foreword

The poem is titled "The Great Lover," and in it writer Rupert Brooke talks about his love affair with life. That is what romantic hearts have, a zest for living and for affirmation. For Brooke it was what he called "love's magnificence," and it encompassed all things from "the cool kindliness of sheets, that soon/ Smooth away trouble . . ." to "radiant raindrops couching in cool flowers."

"These I have loved," says Brooke from the depths of a romantic heart. And oh, how I agree with him, with his ability to take his world one romantic moment

at a time. I have been called a hopeless romantic, a phrase I find odd because romantics are never without hope, never without cups filled with people they love, things they adore, and times too precious to ever take for granted.

Walk on a misty morning in the fall when dew has christened the world and feel your romantic heart swell. See a child asleep, clean and peaceful, and you, too, are so. Sit in a pew on a marriage day with the air itself music, and know how filled to overflowing a heart can be.

These are the sentiments on the pages of this book, each meant intimately for you. We share them with you as Rupert Brooke shared his exuberance, because we romantics seem to have no choice: Not only do we love, we love with "a passion put to use" as Elizabeth Barrett Browning wrote in "How Do I Love Thee." Her sonnet may be the most romantic thing I have ever read, but in this volume you may find words that speak to you alone. Romantics, enjoy.

Nancy Lindemeyer
Editor-in-Chief, *Victoria* Magazine

Suppose I say *summer,*
write the word "hummingbird,"
put it in an envelope,
take it down the hill
to the box. When you open
my letter you will recall
those days and how much,
just how much, I love you.

Raymond Carver
HUMMINGBIRD *FOR TESS*

Love, unconquerable,
Waster of rich men, keeper
Of warm lights and all-night vigil
In the soft face of a girl:
Sea-wanderer, forest-visitor!
Even the pure immortals cannot escape you,
And mortal man, in his one day's dusk,
Trembles before your glory.

Sophocles

Did he appear

because I fell asleep

thinking of him?

If only I'd known I was dreaming,

I'd never have wakened.

Ono No Komachi

We walked together in the dusk
   To watch the tower grow dimly white,
And saw it lift against the sky
   Its flower of amber light.

You talked of half a hundred things,
   I kept each hurried word you said;
And when at last the hour was full,
   I saw the light turn red.

You did not know the time had come,
   You did not see the sudden flower,
Nor know that in my heart Love's birth
   Was reckoned from that hour.

Sara Teasdale
THE METROPOLITAN TOWER

Half the width of the room was still between them, and neither made any show of moving. Archer was conscious of a curious indifference of her bodily presence: he would hardly have been aware of it if one of the hands she had flung out on the table had not drawn his gaze as on the occasion when, in the little Twenty-third Street house, he had kept his eye on it in order not to look at her face. Now his imagination spun about the hand as about the edge of a vortex; but still he made no effort to draw nearer. He had known the love that is fed on caresses and feeds them; but this passion that was closer than his bones was not to be superficially satisfied. His one terror was to do anything which might efface the sound and impression of her words; his one thought, that he should never again feel quite alone.

Edith Wharton

THE AGE OF INNOCENCE

My heart was already
fattening up at the sight of him.

Joyce Carol Oates
WONDERLAND

Falling in Love

The only thing which is not purely mechanical
about falling in love is its beginning.
Although all those who fall in love do so in the same way,
not all fall in love for the same reason.
There is no single quality which is universally loved.

José Ortega y Gasset

nd so, night after night, she would be taken home in Swann's carriage; and one night, after she had got down, and while he stood at the gate and murmured "Till to-morrow, then!" she turned impulsively from him, plucked a last lingering chrysanthemum in the tiny garden which flanked the pathway from the street to her house, and as he went back to his carriage thrust it into his hand. He held it pressed to his lips during the drive home, and when, in due course, the flower withered, locked it away, like something very precious, in a secret drawer of his desk.

Marcel Proust
SWANN'S WAY

hey sang in voices that were so much a part of Africa, so quick to blend with the night and the tranquil veldt and the labyrinths of forest that made their background, that the music seemed without sound. It was like a voice upon another voice, each of the same timbre.

The young men and the girls together stood in a wide circle with their arms on each other's shoulders. The white light of the moon bathed their black bodies, making them blacker. A leader stood alone in the centre of the ring and began the chant; he struck the spark of their song and it caught on the tinder of their youth and ran around the ring like a flame. It was a song of love ~ of this man's love and of that one's. It was a song that changed as many times as there were young men to proclaim their manhood, and lasted as long as there were young girls to trill their applause.

Beryl Markham

WEST WITH THE NIGHT

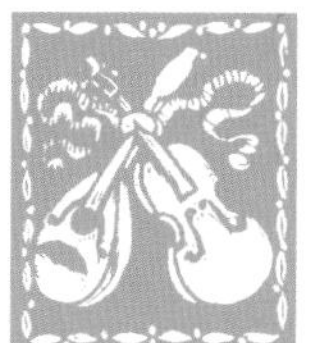

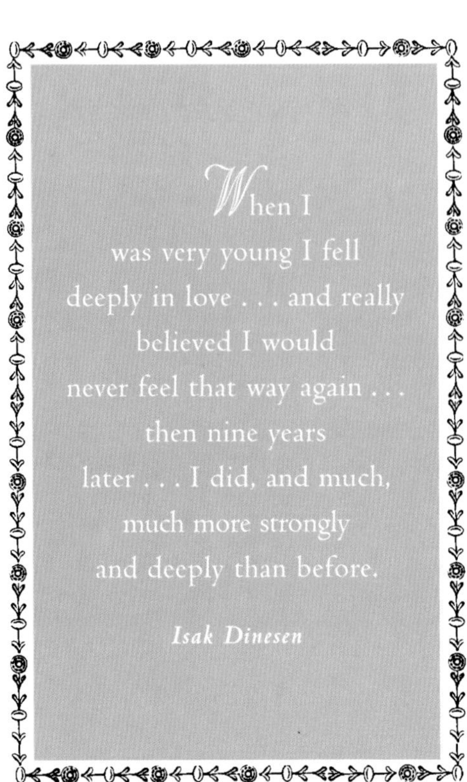
When I
was very young I fell
deeply in love . . . and really
believed I would
never feel that way again . . .
then nine years
later . . . I did, and much,
much more strongly
and deeply than before.
Isak Dinesen

man of the Empire, accustomed to Empire manners, could know nothing at all of the conventions of modern love, the new fashionable scruples, the different mode of conversation invented since 1830, in which the poor weak woman succeeds in being accepted as the victim of her lover's desires, a kind of sister of charity binding up wounds, a self-sacrificing angel. This new art of love uses an enormous number of evangelical phrases in the devil's work. Passion, for example, is a martyrdom. One aspires towards the ideal, the infinite. Both parties desire to be refined through love. All these fine phrases are a pretext for heaping fuel on the flames, adding more ardour to the act, more frenzy to the fall, than in the past. This hypocrisy, characteristic of our times, has corrupted gallantry. A pair of lovers profess to be two angels, and behave like two demons if they have a chance.

Honoré de Balzac
COUSIN BETTE

If I can merit you by a love so chaste and illimitable as ever made the breast of man its tenement, you are mine already, my dear Miss Somersdown. . . . Heaven knows the purity of my intent and the affection which dictates it. . . . Your life of love with me shall be as near an approach to the utmost height of enjoyment as my pecuniary competence, my untiring zeal and infinite affection can make it. . . .

COURTSHIP AS IT IS AND AS IT OUGHT TO BE (1877)

How they rouse every tender sensation of my Soul, which sometimes find vent at my Eyes nor dare I discribe [sic] how earnestly I long to fold to my fluttering Heart the dear object of my warmest affections. The Idea sooths [sic] me, I feast upon it with a pleasure known only to those whose Hearts and hopes are one.

Abigail Adams,
to her husband, John Adams

To love is good, too: love being difficult. For one human being to love another: that is perhaps the most difficult of all our tasks, the ultimate, the last test and proof, the work for which all other work is but preparation.

Rainer Maria Rilke
LETTERS TO A YOUNG POET

Love Stories of My Family

Come walk with me,
There's only thee
To bless my spirit now . . .
So closer would my feelings twine
Because they have no stay but thine.

Emily Brontë

mma's colour was heightened by this unjust praise; and with a smile and shake of the head, which spoke much, she looked at Mr. Knightley. It seemed as if there were an instantaneous impression in her favour, as if his eyes received the truth from hers, and all that had passed of good in her feelings were at once caught and honoured. He looked at her with a glow of regard. She was warmly gratified ~ and in another moment still more so, by a little movement of more than common friendliness on his part. He took her hand; whether she had not herself made the first motion, she could not say ~ she might, perhaps, have rather offered it ~ but he took her hand, pressed it, and certainly was on the point of carrying it to his lips ~ when, from some fancy or other, he suddenly let it go. Why he should feel such a scruple, why he should change his mind when it was all but done, she could not perceive. He would have judged better, she thought, if he had not stopped. The intention, however, was indubitable; and whether it was that his manners had in general so little gallantry, or however else it happened, but she thought nothing became him more. It was with him of so simple, yet so dignified a nature. She could not but recall the attempt with great satisfaction. It spoke such perfect amity.

Jane Austen
EMMA

*With a quick and eager step
did Robin pass through the glades, for
he was going to see the lady he
loved best in all the world. Fair Marian
was she called, the daughter of
Richard FitzWalter of Malaset. Ever
since when, as a boy, Robin had
shot and sported in Locksley Chase, near
where he had been born, Marian
had been his playmate, and though she was
an earl's daughter, and Robin was
but a yeoman and not rich, they had
loved each other dearly, and sworn that
neither would marry anyone else.*

Henry Gilbert
ROBIN HOOD

Laura reached out and touched Ward's cheek, very gently. His skin was warm and smooth. She traced the line of the stain. His face, beneath her hand, was mysterious, closed to her. With the sense of freedom came another realization: she could choose Ward or not, herself. It was not only his decision. And, freed, she knew now what she wanted.

"I love you," she said.

Roxana Robinson
SUMMER LIGHT

Dearest, ~ I wish I had the gift of making rhymes, for methinks there is poetry in my head and heart since I have been in love with you. You are a Poem. Of what sort, then? Epic? Mercy on me, no! A sonnet? No; for that is too labored and artificial. You are a sort of sweet, simple, gay, pathetic ballad, which Nature is singing, sometimes with tears, sometimes with smiles, and sometimes with intermingled smiles and tears.

Nathaniel Hawthorne,
to Sophia Peabody

Tutti
sul A

I Love You

It is the heart, and not the brain,
That to the highest doth attain,
And he who followeth Love's behest
Far excelleth all the rest!

Henry Wadsworth Longfellow
THE BUILDING OF THE SHIP

Gifts That Speak of Love

Never yet deceived by a fiery glance.
Hold the man's heart in your unknowing child-fingers,
draw the man's radiant fire into the icy chamber of your eyes.
You are certain of love as you are of heaven.
He will offer you his heart, an empire, and all the spring flowers,
and you give him the light veil of your longing which turns the distance blue.
Your breath has not yet touched the flickering light of his bliss.
Your eye has not yet measured the breadth of his loyalty.
Your feet have not yet stepped into the closed circle of his fate;
you still do not care whether he is red or blue.
But the day will come when you cling tight
to him like a flower to its stalk,
when his twilight is your light and his drought is your well,
when you wander about in the passages of a vast castle and know that you love

Edith Södergran
TO A YOUNG WOMAN

Sometimes she smiled, allowing her eyes to rest on him for a moment. Then he felt her gaze penetrating as a bright ray of sun reaches to the bottom of the water. He loved her without reservation, without hope of his affection being returned, absolutely; and, in these moments of silent ecstasy which resembled transports of gratitude, he would have liked to cover her forehead with kisses. At the same time he was enraptured by a secret desire; it was a longing to sacrifice himself, a wish to consecrate himself to her immediately, all the stronger for being impossible to fulfill.

Gustave Flaubert
THE SENTIMENTAL EDUCATION

The Qualities of Love

Only God, my dear,
Could love you for yourself alone
And not your yellow hair.

William Butler Yeats,
to Anne Gregory

To me, fair friend, you never can be old,
For as you were when first your eye I ey'd,
Such seems your beauty still.

William Shakespeare
SONNETS (104)

It is a common enough case, that of a man being suddenly captivated by a woman nearly the opposite of his ideal.

George Eliot

To be loved, be lovable.

Ovid

ARS AMATORIA

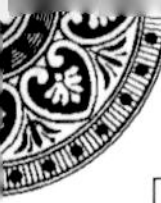

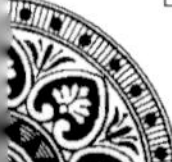

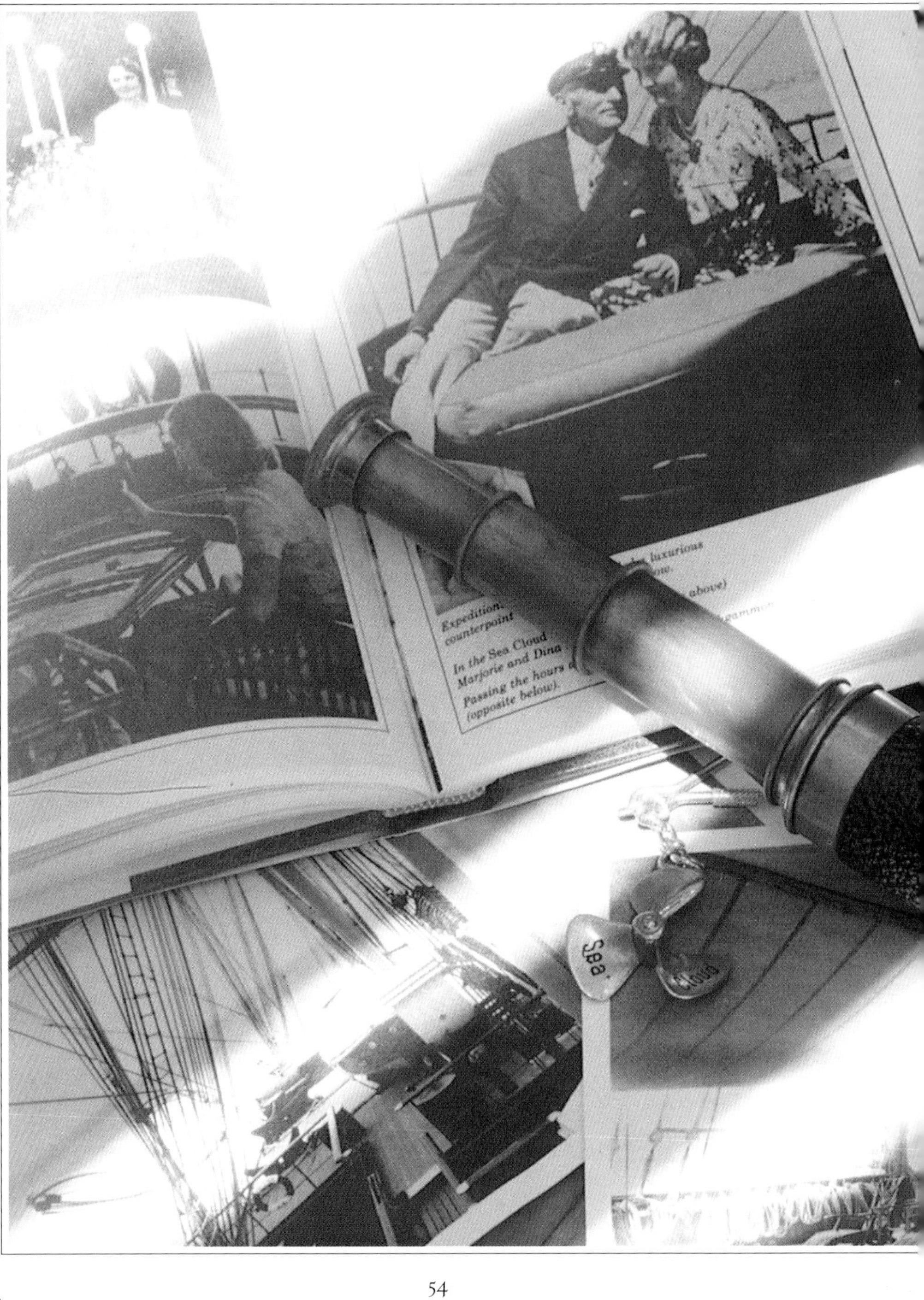
luxurious
above)
Expedition
counterpoint
In the Sea Cloud
Marjorie and Dina
Passing the hours
(opposite below).
Sea
Cloud

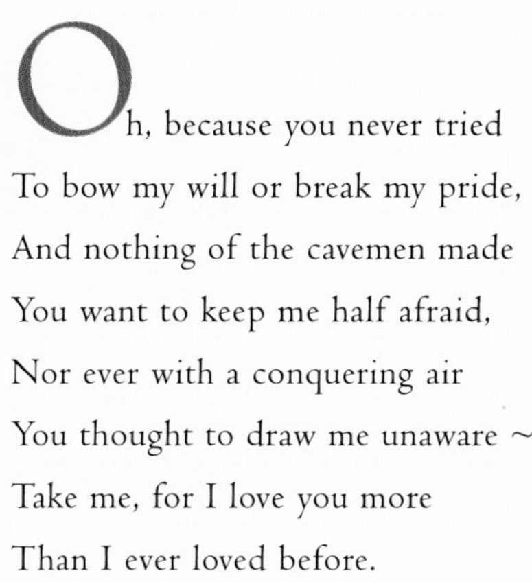

Oh, because you never tried
To bow my will or break my pride,
And nothing of the cavemen made
You want to keep me half afraid,
Nor ever with a conquering air
You thought to draw me unaware ~
Take me, for I love you more
Than I ever loved before.

And since the body's maidenhood
Alone were neither rare nor good
Unless with it I gave to you
A spirit still untrammeled, too,
Take my dreams and take my mind
That were masterless as wind;
And "Master!" I shall say to you
Since you never asked me to.

Sara Teasdale
BECAUSE

He himself
Sought with his lyre of hollow tortoiseshell
To soothe his love-sick heart, and you, sweet wife,
You on the desolate shore alone he sang,
You at return, you at decline of day.

Virgil

It was certainly proposing under difficulties, for, even if he had desired to do so, Mr. Bhaer could not go down upon his knees, on account of the mud; neither could he offer Jo his hand, except figuratively, for both were full; much less could he indulge in tender demonstrations in the open street, though he was near it: so the only way in which he could express his rapture was to look at her, with an expression which glorified his face to such a degree that there actually seemed to be little rainbows in the drops that sparkled on his beard. If he had not loved Jo very much, I don't think he could have done it *then,* for she looked far from lovely, with her skirts in a deplorable state, her rubber boots splashed to the ankle, and her bonnet a ruin. Fortunately, Mr. Bhaer considered her the most beautiful woman living.

Louisa May Alcott
LITTLE WOMEN

I'm talking to you."
He drew a long breath.
"I love you so much, Anne,
that without you
I'd have so much less than
nothing that it won't
bear thinking of.
Will you marry me, and
trust me to make something
of my life?"

Helen Hooven Santmyer
"... AND LADIES OF THE CLUB"

"Why do I love" You, Sir?
Because ~
The Wind does not require the Grass
To answer ~ Wherefore when He pass
She cannot keep Her place.

Emily Dickinson

I should like to know what is the proper function of women, if it is not to make reasons for husbands to stay at home, and still stronger reasons for bachelors to go out.

George Eliot

There is nothing held so dear
As love, if only it be hard to win.
The roses that in yonder hedge appear
Outdo our garden-buds which bloom within;
But since the hand may pluck them every day,
Unmarked they bud, bloom, drop, and drift away.

Jean Ingelow
THERE IS NOTHING HELD SO DEAR

True love is like seeing ghosts:
we all talk about it, but few of us have ever seen one.

La Rochefoucauld

Favorite Love Poems

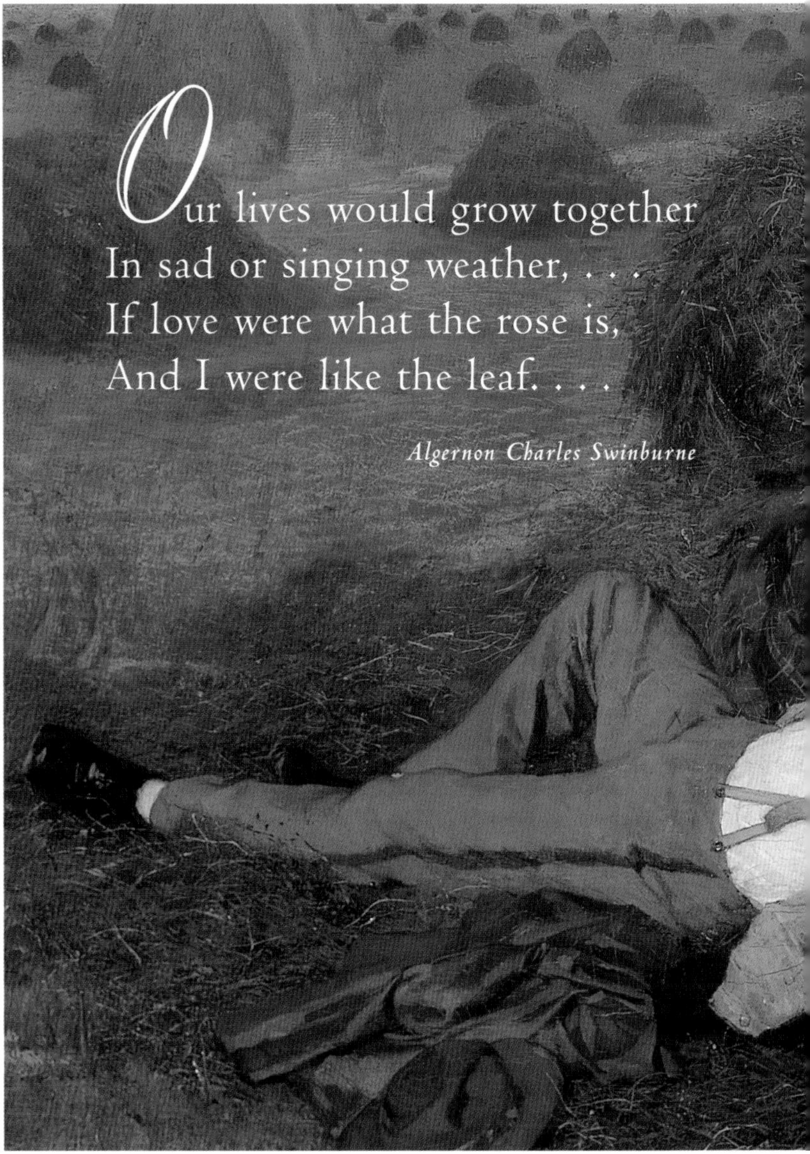

Our lives would grow together
In sad or singing weather, . . .
If love were what the rose is,
And I were like the leaf. . . .

Algernon Charles Swinburne

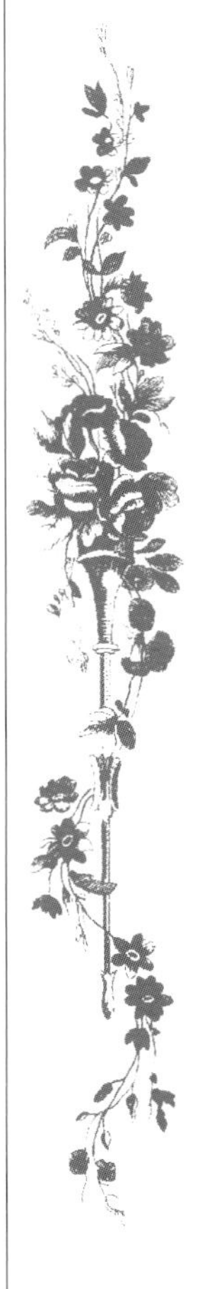

I look down the tracks and see you coming ~ and out of every haze & mist your darling rumpled trousers are hurrying to me ~ Without you, dearest dearest I couldn't see or hear or feel or think ~ or live ~ I love you so and I'm never in all our lives going to let us be apart another night. It's like begging for mercy of a storm or killing Beauty or growing old, without you. I want to kiss you so ~ and in the back where your dear hair starts and your chest ~ I love you ~ and I cant [sic] tell you how much ~

Lover, Lover, Darling ~
Your Wife

Zelda Fitzgerald

"When you loved me, I gave you
the whole sun and stars to play with . . .
and the volume of all
the seas in one impulse of your soul."

George Bernard Shaw
GETTING MARRIED

Fast-anchor'd eternal O love! O woman I love!
O bride! O wife! more resistless than I can tell, the thought of you!

Walt Whitman

Dear Heart,

I know of no other husband in the world who could stand at the train station and wave his wife and family such a dear, brave good-bye.
For one brief moment I wanted to pull the emergency cord and run back into your arms ~ but our reunion will be even sweeter in September.

Elizabeth Forsythe Hailey
A WOMAN OF INDEPENDENT MEANS

You will find, as you look
back upon your life, that the moments
that stand out, the moments
when you have really lived, are the
moments when you have
done things in the spirit of Love.

Henry Drummond

My sweet Girl,
Your Letter gave me more delight, than any thing in the world but you yourself could do; indeed I am almost astonished that any absent one should have that luxurious power over my senses which I feel. Even when I am not thinking of you I recieve your influence and a tenderer nature steeling upon me.

John Keats,
to Fanny Brawne

Love Letters

I confess that I love him ~
I rejoice that I love him ~
I thank the maker of Heaven and Earth ~
that gave him me to love ~
the exultation floods me.

Emily Dickinson,
to Otis P. Lord

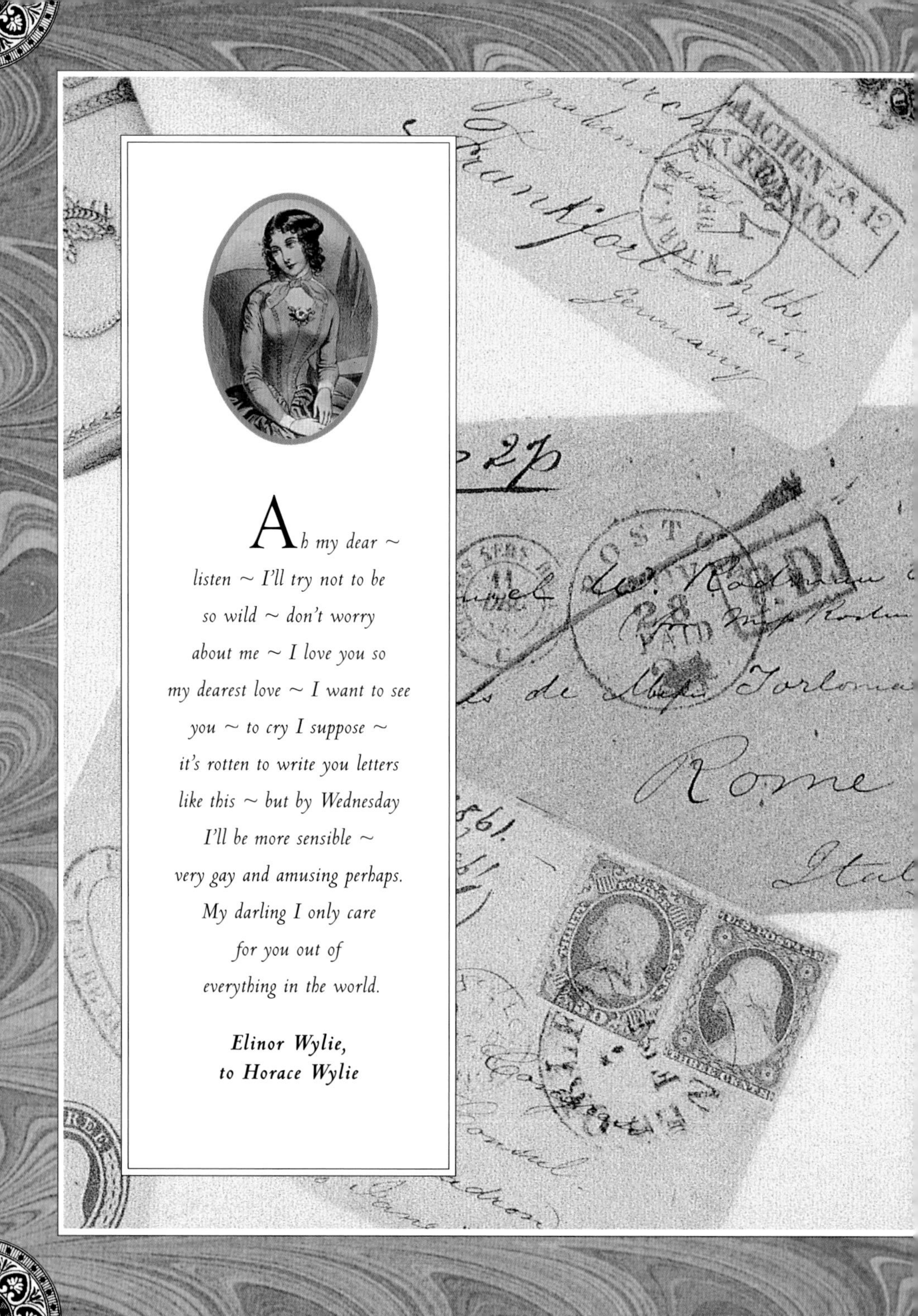

Ah my dear ~
listen ~ I'll try not to be
so wild ~ don't worry
about me ~ I love you so
my dearest love ~ I want to see
you ~ to cry I suppose ~
it's rotten to write you letters
like this ~ but by Wednesday
I'll be more sensible ~
very gay and amusing perhaps.
My darling I only care
for you out of
everything in the world.

Elinor Wylie,
to Horace Wylie

Green Island, N. Y.

My love

I've had three letters from you today: a little note from the 5th, informing me of a first transfer; a charming letter of the 6th, in which you describe how you're all alone in a village emptied of soldiers ~ I could really feel how it must have looked; and lastly the letter of the 7th, in which you inform me of a further transfer to an evacuated village. So it's over, there's no more hope. I've felt terribly agitated all day long ~ as I have, in fact, all these last days ~ but now all of a sudden I'm regaining a kind of peace, my will's uncoupled and my resignation total. My love, my love, how hard it is to be far away from you! I love you so passionately, I'm in floods of tears ~ but tears of love more than sorrow. You wrote to me so tenderly, my sweet little one, my dear little one, my love! It's the first time this evening that I fully realize I'm going to be living without you. That it's going to be a long, long time before I see you ~ I'd thought that impossible. Without you ~ I can't bear the idea. Yourself, my other self, o dear little being, I love you quite desperately.

Simone de Beauvoir,
to Jean-Paul Sartre

Such then are my flights of fancy when, weary of writing, I think of the rare perfection of her who was at birth so aptly named Eve, for she is unique on earth; there cannot be another so angelic, no other woman who could embody more gentleness, more ingenuity, more love, more inspiration in her caresses.

Honoré de Balzac,
to Countess Hanska

The Music of Romance

When the autumn tinged the greenwood,
Turning all its leaves to gold,
In the lawn by the elders shaded,
I my love to Nellie told;
As we stood together, gazing
On the star-bespangled dome,
How I blessed the August evening,
When I saw sweet Nellie home.

TRADITIONAL SONG, 1858

He had loved that shiver, that spasm she could not control; for love must attach to what we cannot help ~ the involuntary, the telltale, the fatal. Otherwise, the reasonableness and the mercy that would make our lives decent and orderly would overpower love, crush it, root it out, tumble it away like a striped tent pegged in sand.

Time passed. By sunlight, by a window, he suddenly saw a web, a radiating system, of wrinkles spread out from the corners of her eyes when she smiled. From her lips another set of creases, so delicate only the sun could trace them, spread upward; the two systems commingled on her cheeks. Time was interconnecting her features, which had been isolated in the spaces of her face by a certain absentminded perfection. She was growing old within their love, within their suffering.

John Updike
from PROBLEMS AND OTHER STORIES

Shut up the door: who loves me must not look
Upon the withered world, but haste to bring
His lighted candle, and his story-book,
And live with me the poetry of Spring.

Alice Cary
AUTUMN

In love, there is always one who kisses and one who offers the cheek.

French Proverb

Men always want to be a woman's first love,
women like to be a man's last romance.

Oscar Wilde

My bounty is as boundless as the sea,
My love as deep; the more I give to thee,
The more I have, for both are infinite.

William Shakespeare
ROMEO AND JULIET

"Many waters cannot quench love," she whispered. "Neither can the floods drown it."

Madeleine L'Engle
MANY WATERS

My face in thine eye, thine in mine appears,
And true plain hearts do in the faces rest.
Where can we find two better hemispheres,
Without sharp north, without declining west?
Whatever dies was not mixed equally;
If our two loves be one, or thou and I
Love so alike that none do slacken, none can die.

John Donne
THE GOOD MORROW

O, my beloved, . . . My morning and my
evening star of love! . . . Even thus,
As that fair planet in the sky above,
Dost thou retire unto thy rest at night,
And from thy darkened window fades the light.

Henry Wadsworth Longfellow

THE EVENING STAR

Ah, love, ~ you are my unutterable blessing.
. . . I am in full sunshine now.

Robert Browning, to his wife,
Elizabeth Barrett Browning

But true love is a durable fire,
In the mind ever burning,
Never sick, never old, never dead,
From itself never turning.

Sir Walter Raleigh
AS YOU CAME FROM THE HOLY LAND

Memories to Cherish

Even if I now saw you
only once,
I would long for you
through worlds,
worlds.

Izumi Shikibu

To the bridge of love,
old stone between tall cliffs
~ eternal meeting place, red evening ~,
I come with my heart.
~ My beloved is only water,
that always passes away, and does not deceive,
that always passes away, and does not change,
that always passes away, and does not end.

Juan Ramón Jiménez
ETERNIDADES

I did love him,
alas too tenderly ~ we lived together
on such terms as man and wife
ought to live, placing perfect confidence
in each other, bearing one another's
burdens and making due allowances for
human imperfection.

Diary of Sarah Ripley Stearns

And I loved you, Ana, don't think I ever forgot that time we went walking in Holguín, even if it was a long, long time ago. We walked so far from your parents' house . . . headed for the park, and whenever we passed through the shadows, where no one could see us, your hand tightened around mine and the air around us seemed charged and then we'd kiss. We stole only a few kisses, I never saw you after that, but don't you ever think that memory has left me, memory of youth and loveliness, how often I've wondered the way things might have been between you and me . . .

Oscar Hijuelos
THE MAMBO KINGS
PLAY SONGS OF LOVE

Their meetings
made December June,
Their every parting
was to die.

Alfred, Lord Tennyson

He who, silent, loves
to be with us ~ he who loves us
in our silence ~ has touched
one of the keys that ravish hearts.

Johann Kaspar Lavater

Love is a talkative passion.

Bishop Wilson

ove is the same as like except you feel sexier. And more romantic. And also more annoyed when he talks with his mouth full. And you also resent it more when he interrupts you. And you also respect him less when he shows any weakness. And furthermore, when you ask him to pick you up at the airport and he tells you he can't do it because he's busy, it's only when you love him that you hate him.

Judith Viorst

Two lovely berries moulded on one stem;
So with two seeming bodies, but one heart.

William Shakespeare
A MIDSUMMER NIGHT'S DREAM

. . . in memoried spring, . . .
her shadowed eyes and lifted throat
Sweetly well with laughter . . .

William Faulkner,
to his future wife

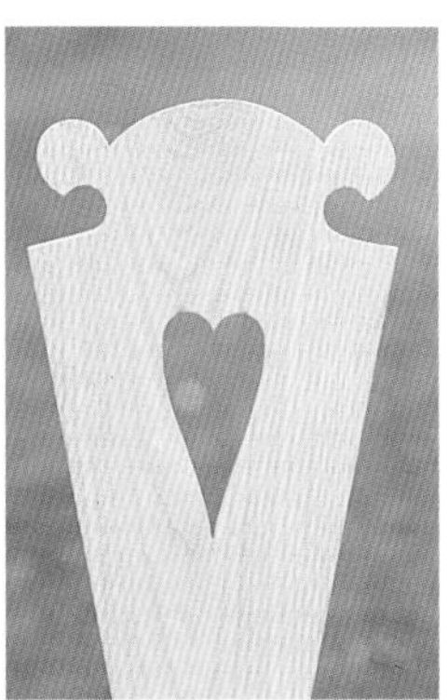

We are not separated
from each other by our differing
experiences but, rather,
in some strange way, closer. Is this
just a miracle of
understanding? Or simply love?
Or do we really both
of us now stand at the same point,
at the end of something,
at the beginning of something?
Both of us are groping and
a little lost ~ but we are together.

Anne Morrow Lindbergh
WAR WITHIN AND WITHOUT

Memories of our time in Italy often come to us and yesterday, as we were walking up a small path, he said softly: "Monte Sacro . . . I owe to you the most beautiful dream of my life."

Lou Andreas-Salomé,
to Frederick Nietzsche

I give you what is unbounded, passing from dark to dark,
containing darkness: a night of rain, an early morning.
I give you the life I have let live for love of you:
a clump of orange-blooming weeds beside the road,
the young orchard waiting in the snow, our own life
that we have planted in this ground, as I
have planted mine in you. I give you my love for all
beautiful and honest women that you gather to yourself
again and again, and satisfy ~ and this poem,
no more mine than any man's who has loved a woman.

Wendell Berry

THE COUNTRY OF MARRIAGE

Years after the war, after marriages, children, divorces, books, he came to Paris with his wife. He phoned her. It's me. She recognized him at once from the voice. He said, I just wanted to hear your voice. She said, It's me, hello. He was nervous, afraid, as before. His voice suddenly trembled. And with the trembling, suddenly, she heard again the voice of China. He knew she'd begun writing books, he'd heard about it through her mother whom he'd met again in Saigon. And about her younger brother, and he'd been grieved for her. Then he didn't know what to say. And then he told her. Told her that it was as before, that he still loved her, he could never stop loving her, that he'd love her until death.

Marguerite Duras
THE LOVER

My grandfather
and grandmother fell in love on
moonlit nights at Saltair.
"I remember the way her chiffon dress
would blow in the breeze as
we stood on the boardwalk looking
over the lake. And I remember a
kiss or two before we went back
inside . . ." he said.

Terry Tempest Williams
REFUGE: AN UNNATURAL HISTORY
OF FAMILY AND PLACE

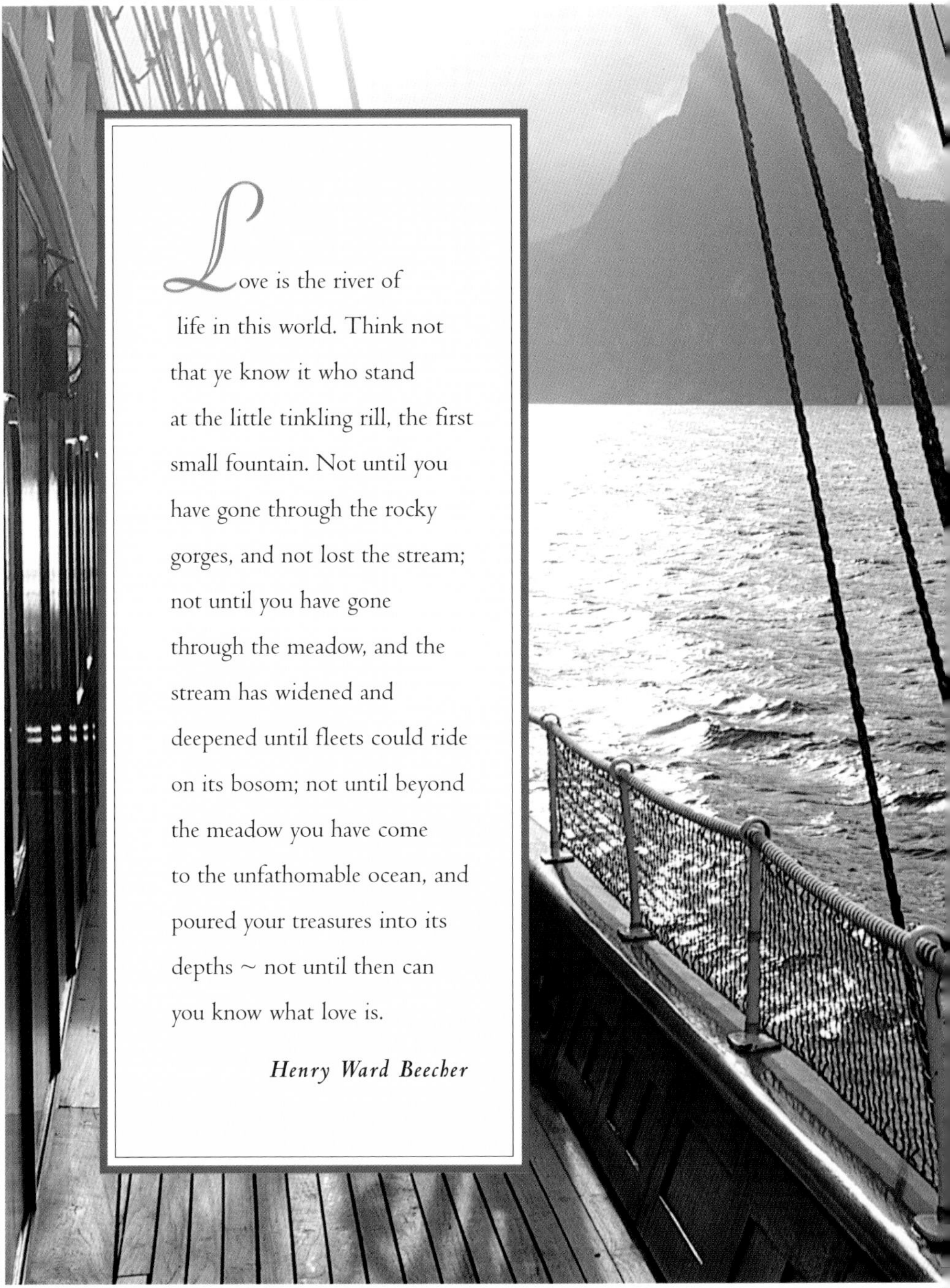

Love is the river of life in this world. Think not that ye know it who stand at the little tinkling rill, the first small fountain. Not until you have gone through the rocky gorges, and not lost the stream; not until you have gone through the meadow, and the stream has widened and deepened until fleets could ride on its bosom; not until beyond the meadow you have come to the unfathomable ocean, and poured your treasures into its depths ~ not until then can you know what love is.

Henry Ward Beecher

PERMISSIONS AND PHOTO CREDITS

Cover and page 87: "My Sweet Rose," painting by John William Waterhouse, courtesy of The Bridgeman Art Library.

7: Photograph by Toshi Otsuki.

8: Photograph from Nina Ovryn Design.

10–11: Photograph by Toshi Otsuki. Excerpt from *A New Path to the Waterfall* by Raymond Carver. Copyright © 1989 by The Estate of Raymond Carver. Used by permission of Grove/Atlantic, Inc.

12: Photograph by Pierre Chanteau.

13: Photograph by Hedrich Blessing.

14–15: Background photograph by Tina Mucci. Inset photograph by William P. Steele. Excerpt from *The Ink Dark Moon: Love Poems* by Ono no Komachi & Izumi Shikibu, translated by Jane Hirshfield. Copyright © 1986, 1987, 1988, 1989, 1990 by Jane Hirshfield. Reprinted by permission of Random House, Inc.

16: Photograph by Luciana Pampalone.

17: Photograph by Tina Mucci.

18: Photograph by Tina Mucci. Excerpt reprinted with the permission of Charles Scribner's Sons, an imprint of Macmillan Publishing, from *The Age of Innocence* by Edith Wharton. Copyright 1920 D. Appleton & Co.; copyright renewed 1948 William R. Tyler.

19: Photograph by Hedrich Blessing.

20: Photograph by William P. Steele.

22: Photograph by Wendi Schneider.

23: Photograph by Hedrich Blessing.

24: Photograph by Toshi Otsuki.

26: Excerpt from *West with the Night* by Beryl Markham. Copyright

© 1942, 1983 by Beryl Markham. Reprinted by permission of Farrar, Straus & Giroux.

27: Photograph by William P. Steele.

29: Photograph by Toshi Otsuki.

30: Photograph by Toshi Otsuki.

33: "Danse à la ville," painting by Renoir, courtesy of E.T. Archive.

34: Photograph by Toshi Otsuki.

35: Excerpt from *Abigail Adams: A Biography* by Phyllis L. Levin. Copyright © 1987 by Phyllis Lee Levin. Reprinted by permission of St. Martin's Press. Excerpt from *Letters to a Young Poet* by Rainer Maria Rilke; translated by M. D. Herter Norton and reprinted with permission of W. W. Norton & Co., Inc. Copyright © 1934 by W. W. Norton & Co., Inc. Renewed 1962 by M. D. Herter Norton.

36: Photograph by Toshi Otsuki.

37: Photograph by Toshi Otsuki.

39: Photograph by Toshi Otsuki.

41: Photograph by Starr Ockenga.

42–43: Background and inset photographs by Toshi Otsuki. Excerpt from *Summer Light* by Roxana Robinson reprinted with permission of Sterling Lord Literistic, Inc. Copyright © 1988 Roxana Robinson.

44: Photograph from Nina Ovryn Design.

45: Photograph by Hedrich Blessing.

46: Photograph by Pierre Chanteau.

48: "To A Young Woman" by Edith Södergran from *Love and Solitude.* Translation by Stina Katchadourian. Copyright © 1981, 1985, 1992 by Stina Katchadourian. Reprinted with permission of Fjord Press.

49: Photograph by Luciana Pampalone.

51: Photograph by Toshi Otsuki.

53: Photograph from Nina Ovryn Design.

54–55: Photograph by Toshi Otsuki.

57: Photograph by Toshi Otsuki.

58: Photograph by Pierre Chanteau.

60–61: Photograph by Toshi Otsuki. Excerpt from ". . . *And Ladies of the Club*" by Helen Hooven Santmyer. Copyright © 1982. Reprinted by permission of the Ohio State University Press.

62: Photograph by Tina Mucci.

63: Photograph by Toshi Otsuki.

64: Photograph from Nina Ovryn Design.

65: Background photograph by Wendi Schneider. Inset photograph by Toshi Otsuki.

66–67: Photograph by Toshi Otsuki.

68: Photograph by Toshi Otsuki.

70–71: "The Lovers," painting by Merse Pal, courtesy of E.T. Archive.

72: Photograph by Tom Eckerle. Excerpt from *Zelda* by Nancy Milford. Copyright © 1970 by Nancy Wilson Milford. Published by Harper & Row. Reprinted by permission of Brandt & Brandt.

73: Photograph by Tom Eckerle.

74: Photograph by Toshi Otsuki.

75: Photograph by Michael Skott.

76–77: Background photograph by Toshi Otsuki. Inset photograph by Tom Eckerle.

78: From *A Woman of Independent Means* by Elizabeth Forsythe Hailey. Copyright © 1978 by Elizabeth Forsythe Hailey. Used by

permission of Viking Penguin, a division of Penguin Books USA Inc.

79: Photograph by Michael Skott.

80: Photograph by Toshi Otsuki.

81: Photograph by Toshi Otsuki.

82–83: Background photograph by Toshi Otsuki. Inset photograph from Nina Ovryn Design.

84: Photograph by Toshi Otsuki.

86: Excerpt reprinted by permission of the publishers from *The Letters of Emily Dickinson* edited by Thomas H. Johnson, Cambridge, Mass.: The Belknap Press of Harvard University Press, copyright © 1958, 1986 by the President and Fellows of Harvard College.

88–89: Background photograph by Luciana Pampalone. Inset photograph by Starr Ockenga. Excerpt from *Elinor Wylie: A Life Apart* by Stanley Olsen. Copyright © 1979 by Stanley Olsen. Published by Dial Press. Reprinted with permission of the Julian Bach Agency.

90: Photograph by Wendi Schneider.

91: From *Letters to Sartre* by Simone de Beauvoir. Copyright © 1990 by Editions Gallimard. English translation copyright © 1991 by Quintin Hoare. By permission of Little, Brown and Company.

92: Photograph by Toshi Otsuki.

95: Photograph by Toshi Otsuki.

96: Excerpt from "Love Song for a Moog Synthesizer" from *Problems and Other Stories* by John Updike. Copyright © 1972, 1973, 1974, 1975, 1976, 1977, 1978, 1979 by John Updike. Reprinted with permission of Alfred A. Knopf.

97: Background and inset photographs by Toshi Otsuki.

98–99: Photograph by Michael Skott.

100: Photograph by Toshi Otsuki.

101: Photograph by Luciana Pampalone.

102: Photograph by William P. Steele.

103: Photograph by Toshi Otsuki.

104–105: Photograph by Tom Eckerle.

107: Photograph by Wendi Schneider.

108: Photograph by Luciana Pampalone.

109: Photograph by Luciana Pampalone.

110: Photograph by Toshi Otsuki.

112: Photograph from Nina Ovryn Design. Excerpt from *The Ink Dark Moon: Love Poems* by Ono no Komachi & Izumi Shikibu, translated by Jane Hirshfield. Copyright © 1986, 1987, 1988, 1989, 1990 by Jane Hirshfield. Reprinted by permission of Random House, Inc.

113: Photograph by Toshi Otsuki. Excerpt from the James Wright translation of *Eternidades* by Juan Ramón Jiménez. Reprinted from *Collected Poems,* copyright © 1971 by James Wright, Wesleyan University Press. By permission of University Press of New England.

114–115: Photograph by Wendi Schneider.

116: Excerpt from *The Mambo Kings Play Songs of Love* by Oscar Hijuelos. Copyright © 1989 by Oscar Hijuelos. Reprinted by permission of Farrar, Straus & Giroux.

117: Photograph by Wendi Schneider.

118–119: Photograph by Toshi Otsuki.

120: Photograph by Michael Skott.

122–123: Photograph by Tina Mucci.

124: Photograph by Michael Skott.

125: Photograph by Starr Ockenga.

126: Photograph by Toshi Otsuki. Excerpt from *The War Within and Without: Diaries and Letters of Anne Morrow Lindbergh 1939-1944*, copyright © 1980 by Anne Morrow Lindbergh, reprinted by permission of Harcourt, Brace & Company.

127: Photograph by Starr Ockenga.

128–129: Photograph by Toshi Otsuki.

130: Photograph from Nina Ovryn Design. Excerpt from "The Country of Marriage" in *The Country of Marriage*, copyright © 1971 by Wendell Berry, reprinted by permission of Harcourt, Brace & Company.

131: Photograph by Toshi Otsuki.

132–133: Photograph by Tina Mucci. Excerpt from *The Lover* by Marguerite Duras, translated by Barbara Bray. Translation copyright © 1985 by Random House, Inc., and William Collins Sons & Co., Ltd. Reprinted by permission of Pantheon Books, a division of Random House, Inc.

134: Photograph by Wendi Schneider.

135: Excerpt from *The Refuge* by Terry Tempest Williams. Copyright © 1991 Terry Tempest Williams. Reprinted by permission of Random House, Inc.

136–137: Photograph by Toshi Otsuki.

144: Photograph by Toshi Otsuki.